BRITISH RAILWAYS
STEAMING
THROUGH
THE SIXTIES

Volume Fifteen

Compiled by
PETER HANDS

DEFIANT PUBLICATIONS
190 Yoxall Road,
Shirley, Solihull,
West Midlands

Printed on behalf of Richard Netherwood Ltd., by Gorenjski tisk p.o. Slovenia.

CURRENT STEAM PHOTOGRAPH ALBUMS AVAILABLE
FROM DEFIANT PUBLICATIONS

VOLUME 14
A4 size - Hardback. 96 pages
-178 b/w photographs.
£14.95 + £1.50 postage.
ISBN 0 946857 40 7.

VOLUME 15
A4 size - Hardback. 96 pages
-178 b/w photographs.
£16.95 + £1.50 postage.
ISBN 0 946857 52 0.

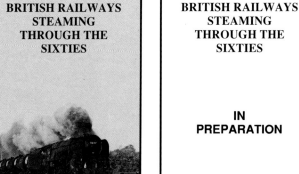

BRITISH RAILWAYS STEAMING THROUGH THE SIXTIES

IN PREPARATION

VOLUME 16

VOLUME 1
A4 size - Hardback. 96 pages
-177 b/w photographs.
£14.95 + £1.50 postage.
ISBN 0 946857 41 5.

VOLUME 9
A4 size - Hardback. 96 pages
-177 b/w photographs.
£14.95 + £1.50 postage.
ISBN 0 946857 37 7.

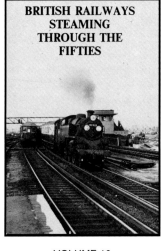

VOLUME 10
A4 size - Hardback. 96 pages
-176 b/w photographs.
£14.95 + £1.50 postage.
ISBN 0 946857 38 5.

VOLUME 11
A4 size - Hardback. 96 pages
-176 b/w photographs.
£16.95 + £1.50 postage.
ISBN 0 946857 48 2.

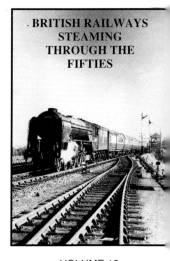

VOLUME 12
A4 size - Hardback. 96 pages
-176 b/w photographs.
£16.95 + £1.50 postage.
ISBN 0 946857 49 0.

VOLUME 1
A4 size - Hardback. 96 pages
-177 b/w photographs.
£14.95 + £1.50 postage.
ISBN 0 946857 39 3.

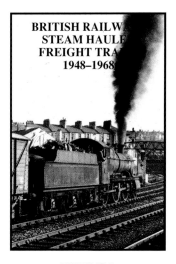

VOLUME 1
A4 size - Hardback. 96 pages
-174 b/w photographs.
£14.95 + £1.50 postage.
ISBN 0 946857 42 3.

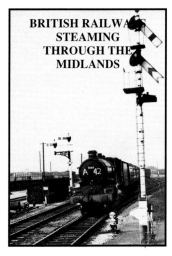

VOLUME 1
A4 size - Hardback. 96 pages
-179 b/w photographs.
£15.95 + £1.50 postage.
ISBN 0 946857 43 I.

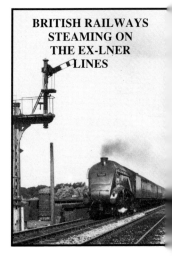

VOLUME 3
A4 size - Hardback. 96 pages
-183 b/w photographs.
£15.95 + £1.50 postage.
ISBN 0 946857 44 X.

FUTURE STEAM PHOTOGRAPH ALBUMS
AND OTHER TITLES

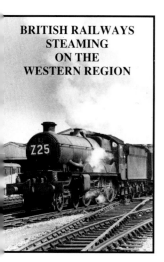

BRITISH RAILWAYS STEAMING ON THE WESTERN REGION

VOLUME 4
A4 size - Hardback. 96 pages
177 b/w photographs.
£15.95 + £1.50 postage.
ISBN 0 946857 46 6.

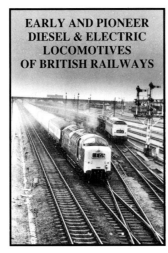

EARLY AND PIONEER DIESEL & ELECTRIC LOCOMOTIVES OF BRITISH RAILWAYS

A4 size - Hardback. 96 pages
-177 b/w photographs.
£15.95 + £1.50 postage.
ISBN 0 946857 45 8.

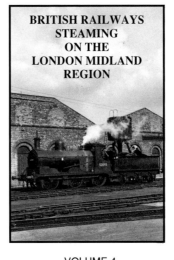

BRITISH RAILWAYS STEAMING ON THE LONDON MIDLAND REGION

VOLUME 4
A4 size - Hardback. 96 pages
-177 b/w photographs.
£15.95 + £1.50 postage.
ISBN 0 946857 47 4.

BRITISH RAILWAYS STEAMING ON THE SOUTHERN REGION

IN PREPARATION

VOLUME 3

BRITISH RAILWAYS STEAM HAULED TITLED TRAINS

A4 size - Hardback. 96 pages
169 b/w photographs.
16.95 + £1.50 postage.
ISBN 0 946857 51 2.

BRITISH RAILWAYS STEAMING THROUGH CREWE, DONCASTER, EASTLEIGH AND SWINDON

IN PREPARATION

BRITISH RAILWAYS STEAMING THROUGH LONDON

IN PREPARATION

BRITISH RAILWAYS STEAMING ON THE EX-LNER LINES

IN PREPARATION

VOLUME 4

BRITISH RAILWAYS STEAMING FROM 1948–1968

'50th' ALBUM
A4 size - Hardback. 96 pages
86 b/w photographs.
16.95 + £1.50 postage.
ISBN 0 946857 50 4.

BRITISH RAILWAYS STEAM HAULED PASSENGER TRAINS IN THE FIFTIES

IN PREPARATION

VOLUME 2

BRITISH RAILWAYS STEAM HAULED PASSENGER TRAINS IN THE SIXTIES

IN PREPARATION

VOLUME 2

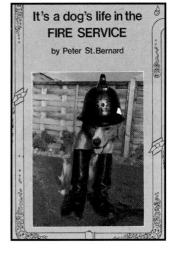

It's a dog's life in the **FIRE SERVICE**
by Peter St.Bernard

COMEDY
269 pages. Cartoons.
£9.95 + £1.00 postage.
ISBN 0 946857 30 X.

ACKNOWLEDGEMENTS

Grateful thanks are.exlended to the following contributors not only for their use in this book but for their kind patience and long term loan of negatives/photographs whilst this book was being compiled.

T.R.AMOS TAMWORTH	G.D.APPLEYARD MIDDLESBROUGH	B.J.ASHWORTH PENTYRCH
W.BOYDEN BEXHILL	P.A.BRIDGMAN HUCCLECOTE	N.L.BROWNE ALDERSHOT
R.BUTTERFIELD MIRFIELD	R.S.CARPENTER BIRMINGHAM	KEN ELLIS SWINDON
TIM FAREBROTHER BOURTON	B.K.B.GREEN WARRINGTON	R.W.HINTON GLOUCESTER
H.L.HOLLAND ST.CATHERINES, ONTARIO, CANADA	F.HORNBY NORTH CHEAM	A.C.INGRAM WISBECH
A.JONES BATH	D.K.JONES MOUNTAIN ASH	B.J.MILLER BARRY
T.NICHOLLS BRISTOL	A.F.NISBET BRACKLEY	R.PICTON WOLVERHAMPTON
W.PIGGOTT UNKNOWN	W.POTTER BISHOPS CLEEVE	N.E.PREEDY HUCCLECOTE
A.RANKIN BARRHEAD	C.RICHARDS SOLIHULL	J.SCHATZ LITTLETHORPE
K.L.SEAL ANDOVERSFORD	JOHN SMITH LENS OF SUTTON	C.P.STACEY STONY STRATFORD
M.S.STOKES MARPLE	D.TITHERIDGE FAREHAM	J.M.TOLSON BIGGLESWADE
G.H.TRURAN GLASTONBURY	R.TURNER SHEFFIELD	D.WEBSTER *
KIT WINDLE LOWER BREDBURY	J.WRAITHMELL MIRFIELD	MIKE WOOD BIRMINGHAM

*Courtesy of the Norman Preedy Collection.

Front Cover - BR Class 9F 2-10-0 No 92137, from 21A Saltley, powers its way along near to Stonehouse, between Gloucester and Bristol with a train of empty oil tanks from Bromford Bridge, Birmingham to Fawley in the summer of 1961. No 92137 was drafted away from Saltley in August 1966 to 6C Croes Newydd. (P.A.Bridgman)

ISBN 0 946857 52 0

© P.B.HANDS 1995
FIRST PUBLISHED 1995

INTRODUCTION

BRITISH RAILWAYS STEAMING THROUGH THE SIXTIES - Volume Fifteen is the fifteenth in a series of books designed to give the ordinary, everyday steam photographic enthusiast of the 1960's a chance to participate in and give pleasure to others whilst recapturing the twilight days of steam.

In this series, wherever possible, no famous names will be found nor will photographs which have been published before be used. The photographs chosen have been carefully selected to give a mixture of action and shed scenes from many parts of British Railways whilst utilising a balanced cross-section of locomotives of GWR, SR, LMS, LNER & BR origins.

As steam declined, especially from 1966 onwards, the choice of locomotive classes and locations also dwindled. Rather than include the nowadays more traditional preserved locomotives in the latter days of steam, the reader will find more locomotives of SR, LMS & BR backgrounds towards the end of the book.

The majority of photographs used in Volume Fifteen have been contributed by readers of Peter Hands series of booklets entitled "What Happened to Steam" & "BR Steam Shed Allocations" and from readers of the earlier "BR Steaming Through the Sixties" albums. In normal circumstances these may have been hidden from the public eye forever.

The continuation of the "BR Steaming" series etc., depends upon *you* the reader. If you wish to join my mailing list for future albums and/or feel you have suitable material of BR steam locomotives between 1948-1968 and wish to contribute them towards this series and other albums, please contact:-

Tel. No.
0121 745-8421

Peter Hands,
190 Yoxall Road,
Shirley, Solihull,
West Midlands B90 3RN

CONTENTS

NAMEPLATES - Nameplate examples of the five main representatives of British Railways.

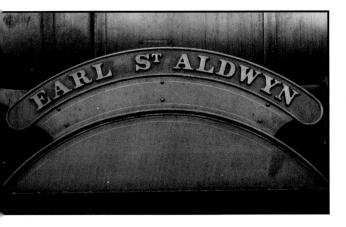

1) GWR *Castle* Class 4-6-0 No 5059 *Earl St. Aldwyn.*
(N.L.Browne)

2) SR *King Arthur* Class 4-6-0 No 30773 *Sir Lavaine.*
(R.Picton)

3) LMS *Jubilee* Class 4-6-0 No 45593 *Kolhapur.* (R.Hinton)

4) LNER A4 Class 4-6-2 No 60034 *Lord Faringdon.*
(R.Butterfield)

5) BR *Britannia* Class 4-6-2 No 70020 *Mercury.* (N.E.Preedy)

6) High pressure steam escapes from the safety valves of SR Unrebuilt *Battle of Britain* Class 4-6-2 No 34056 *Croydon*, from 72A Exmouth Junction, as it stands in front of the wooden built former London and South Western Railway shed at 72E Barnstaple Junction on 24th June 1960. Constructed at Eastleigh Works in February 1947, *Croydon* was rebuilt during December 1960. The depot at Barnstaple Junction closed completely in September 1964. (N.L.Browne) .

7) Conversation time at Inverness on a sun-filled day between a driver and a shunter on 14th July 1960. Former Caledonian Railway McIntosh Class 2P 0-4-4T No 55198, from the nearby shed at 60A, is being employed on station pilot duties. Once based at 63C Forfar, No 55198 had been transferred to Inverness in October 1958 where it worked until withdrawal in May 1961. After a lengthy period of storage it was sent to Inverurie Works for scrapping. (N.E.Preedy)

8) By May 1960 overhauls to steam locomotives were still in full swing at Swindon Works on the Western Region despite the ever increasing ranks of diesel locomotives. Ex. works at the end of the month and awaiting the order to be steamed are GWR 7200 Class 2-8-0T No 7253, from 86A Newport (Ebbw Junction), and GWR *Castle* Class 4-6-0 No 7008 *Swansea Castle*, an inmate of 81A Old Oak Common, which had been equipped with a double chimney in May 1959. (D.K.Jones)

9) Looking in fine external fettle, SR C2X Class 0-6-0 No 32449 stands in the yard of its home shed at 75A Brighton on 24th April 1960. Behind the locomotive the former workshops can be seen. Originally built for the London Brighton and South Coast Railway in 1894 as a C2 goods 0-6-0 by Robert Billinton, it was reboilered in 1912 with an extended smokebox by Marsh. It survived in traffic until June 1961, being withdrawn from 75E Three Bridges. (Tim Farebrother)

10) Rendered surplus to operating requirements by the growing fleet of diesels in Scotland, LNER D49 Class 4-4-0 No 62749 *The Cleveland* has been cast to one side on a dead road at its former power base of 64B Haymarket in May 1960. One of a batch of locomotives from the 'Hunt' series of D49's, *The Cleveland* made a last sad journey to Darlington Works during this same month and was stored there until summoned by the cutter in July 1960. (A.Rankin)

11) The huge ornate roof at London's Victoria station is supported by row upon row of load bearing cast iron pillars as BR Class 4 2-6-4T No 80011 simmers within its confines on 20th April 1960 after arriving with a local passenger from East Grinstead, consisting of a mixed bag of coaching stock. Based at 75E Three Bridges, No 80011 remained there until January 1963. Built at Brighton these large engines worked all over the BR system. (Tim Farebrother)

12) The GWR *Grange* Class 4-6-0's differed from the *Hall* Class 4-6-0's only in wheel diameter and other minor details such as raised frames over the cylinders. On 14th May 1960 No 6876 *Kingsland Grange*, from 86A Newport (Ebbw Junction) coupled with a 3,500 gallon tender, passes through former Midland Railway Territory at Defford with a Newport to Stourbridge freight. *Kingsland Grange* was withdrawn from 85A Worcester in November 1965. (Tim Farebrother)

13) A lower quadrant signal arm bows its head and allows a clear path for LMS Ivatt Class 4 'Flying Pig' 2-6-0 No 43013 (21A Saltley) as it passes the remains of Tewkesbury Junction with an afternoon passenger service from Birmingham (New Street) to Malvern in the summer of 1960. In the left of the frame is the remnants of the signalbox and above the tender of No 43013 we can see the water tower once used for engines working the Malvern to Ashchurch line. (Tim Farebrother)

14) Designed at Doncaster Works and shedded at 75B Redhill, BR Class 4 2-6-0 No 76055 is hemmed between a small diesel shunter and an unidentified SR K Class 2-6-0 at 75A Brighton in April 1960. Due to the lack of water troughs on the Southern Region, No 76055, in common with other types, is fitted with a larger capacity tender. It was drafted to 72B Salisbury the following month and ended its days at 70D Eastleigh in October 1965. (Tim Farebrother)

5) A splendid panoramic view over a section of London with a large power station dominating the background on 9th July 1960. One of a batch of GWR 5700 Class 0-6-0 Pannier Tanks allocated to 70A Nine Elms, No 9770 arrives at Clapham Junction with empty coaching stock from Waterloo where we are looking over the western approach to the Windsor line platfoms. No 9770 moved back to the Western Region in July 1963, to 82F Bath Green Park. (N.L.Browne)

6) A rarity from the North Eastern Region, LNER K3 Class 2-6-0 No 61853, from 56B Ardsley, pilots a filthy 82E Bristol Barrow Road LMS *Jubilee* Class 4-6-0 No 45662 *Kempenfelt* as they race towards Defford with a heavy southbound express from York to Bristol in August 1960. Both of these locomotives were destined to be withdrawn within one month of each other, with *Kempenfelt* going in November 1962 and No 61853 in December. (Tim Farebrother)

11

17) Conversation time at Brookwood station on 13th April 1960 between the footplate crew of SR Rebuilt *West Country* Class 4-6-2 No 34048 *Crediton* (72B Salisbury) and a young trainspotter. Today, the railwaymen may well be long retired, but one wonders about the fortunes of the young lad in future years! *Crediton* started its life Brighton in November 1946 and was rebuilt during March 1959. It is seen at Brookwood on a local service to Waterloo. (Tim Farebrother)

18) The depot yard at 15C Leicester (Midland) is overlooked by a gaunt dwelling on a sunny and warm 26th June 1960. Present and in steam are an unidentified LMS Class 5 4-6-0 and BR Class 9F 2-10-0 No 92121, a resident of Leicester (Midland) since almost brand new in August 1957. It survived in service at 15C/15A until drafted to 8H Birkenhead in April 1965. After condemnation from the same in July 1967 it was cut up at Thompsons, Stockton-on-Tees. (R.W.Hinton)

9) In direct contrast to the 'superpower' seen in the last photograph we espy a diminutive former Caledonian Class 2F 0-6-0T No 56170 in the yard at 66A Polmadie (Glasgow) on 20th April 1960. It is the end of the road for No 56170, having being once based at 65G Yoker, 65E Kipps and latterly from 66D Greenock prior to withdrawal a couple of months before this photograph was taken. Cutting up came at Inverurie Works later in the year. (N.E.Preedy)

0) During 1960 Malvern Wells played host to a number of excursions from the north of England which terminated at Great Malvern. Dwarfed by a large wooden-posted lower quadrant, LNER B1 Class 4-6-0 No 61138 is seen approaching Malvern Wells tender-first with a rake of coaches. No 61138 then rested for the afternoon before returning to Sheffield and its home base at 41A Darnall. It remained in the Sheffield area until January 1964. (Tim Farebrother)

21)On 15th March 1960 the driver of GWR 1400 Class 0-4-2T No 1472 (85B Gloucester - Horton Road) enjoys the early spring sunshine as his charge waits patiently at Gloucester (Central) with a local passenger bound for Chalford. Fitted with push and pull apparatus, No 1472 began life as No 4872 in April 1936 at Danygraig shed. Its last base was at Horton Road from where it was withdrawn in November 1964 a month after the Chalford service ceased. (Tim Farebrother)

22) Wickwar, on the former Midland Main Line, situated between Stonehouse and Yate, is the setting for this photograph taken on a summer Saturday in August 1960. 17C Rowsley based BR Caprotti Class 5 4-6-0 No 73142 is about to pass the small signalbox as it departs from Wickwar station (closed in 1965) and heads for Bristol with a southbound express. Like many of its sister locomotives, No 73142 ended its days based at 9H Patricroft. (Ken Ellis)

3) A member of the footplate crew of former Great Central Railway 04/7 Class 2-8-0 No 63858, from 36A Doncaster, goes about his business as his charge rests in the shed yard at 41J Langwith Junction on an unknown day in April 1960. The 04/7 sub-class totalled thirty-four units in all. No 63858 was based briefly at Langwith Junction, from November 1964 to December 1965, before moving back to Doncaster shed from where it was withdrawn in April 1966. (N.E.Preedy)

4) SR Maunsell designed *King Arthur* Class 4-6-0 No 30804 *Sir Cador of Cornwall* stands in steam beside a large supply dump of coal at its home shed at 71A Eastleigh on 26th March 1960. Built at Eastleigh in 1926, *Sir Cador of Cornwall* soldiered on in revenue earning service until February 1962. In the background is BR Class 4 4-6-0 No 75078, from 70D Basingstoke, (withdrawn in July 1966) which has since been preserved on the Keighley & Worth Valley Railway for many years. (F.Hornby)

CHAPTER TWO - 1961

25) Seen here on former Great North of Scotland territory at Keith shed, coded 61C, is LNER Bl Class 4-6-0 No 61308 on 19th May 1961 . At this date in time No 61308 was on the books of 61A Kittybrewster, but during the early part of 1957 it was based at Keith shed. It left 61A a month after this photograph was taken, being transferred to 64A St.Margarets (Edinburgh). Keith shed was used in the late sixties to house stored members of the ill-fated North British built D6100 Class diesels. (N.E.Preedy)

26) A usurper in the camp at Crewe station in November 1961. With the hands of the clock approaching five minutes to four in the afternoon, 84A Wolverhampton (Stafford Road) based GWR 5700 Class 0-6-0PT No 3792 simmers in a bay platform next to a diesel multiple unit not long after arriving with a two coach local passenger train from Wellington. After Stafford Road closed in September 1963, No 3792 moved 'up the road' to 84B Oxley. (Kit Windle)

27) Sulphurous smoke belches from the funnel of BR Class 5 4-6-0 No 73031 as it pollutes the atmosphere at Bristol (Temple Meads) in February 1961. No 73031, from 82E Bristol Barrow Road, was 'officially' allocated to Rugby Testing Station on this date, but for some reason is in charge of an express many miles away from Rugby! In December 1961 it was 'released' from the Testing Station and drafted to 82F Bath Green Park on the former S & D. (D.K.Jones)

28) Although constructed as far back as 1924, LNER A3 Class 4-6-2 No 60049 *Galtee More*, from 34F Grantham, finds pride of place at the head of the down *Northumbrian* at Wood Green on the outskirts of London on 19th April 1961. *Galtee More*, equipped with a double chimney in April 1959 was the first member of the A3 Class to be fitted with the German style of smoke deflectors, in October 1960. It was withdrawn from traffic in December 1962. (T.R.Amos)

29) Allocated to 73A Stewarts Lane in London, SR Rebuilt *West Country* Class 4-6-2 No 34100 *Appledore* finds itself somewhat off the beaten track as it heads a parcels/passenger train at Bournemouth (Central) on 17th September 1961. Once of 74B Ramsgate and later of 75A Brighton and 70E Salisbury, *Appledore* had been rebuilt at Eastleigh Works in September 1960. It was condemned from Salisbury shed in July 1967 and cut up at Cashmores, Newport. (B.K.B.Green)

30) A dull and overcast day at 81A Old Oak Common on 5th November 1961. The imposing building in the background is the multi-road repair shop, in front of which is an unidentified GWR *King* Class 4-6-0 and several 0-6-0 Diesel shunters. In the right of the frame is a member of the *Warship* Class diesel-hydraulics. Centrepiece of this picture is of GWR 6100 Class 2-6-2T No 6111, of 81F Oxford. Despite its forlorn condition it worked until December 1965. (N.L.Browne)

31) A splendid view of BR Class 9F 2-10-0 No 92208, from 88A Cardiff (Canton), as seen alongside the running shed at 84F Stourbridge on 17th September 1961 . Note the WD Class 2-8-0 in the distance. No 92208, introduced into service in June 1958 had a working life of less than nine years before condemnation in October 1967. During its short career it also worked from the sheds at 83D Laira (Plymouth) and 12A Carlisle (Kingmoor) as well as several others. (N.E.Preedy)

32) A miserable and cold looking scene at London Road Junction, Derby during the winter of 1961. Occupying the centre of the frame is a diminutive signalbox a relic of the Midland Railway long since swept away by modernisation. Also long gone, in the left of the frame, is LMS Ivatt Class 4 2-6-0 No 43041, a resident of 21A Saltley, as it heads a freight train in a southbound direction beneath a small overhead gantry of lower quadrant signals. (R.S.Carpenter)

33) Coaled and watered in readiness for its next call to duty, GWR *King* Class 4-6-0 No 6024 *King Edward I*, from 81A Old Oak Common, stands next to a begrimed member of the LMS *Jubilee* Class 4-6-0's at 89A Shrewsbury on an undefined date in 1961. *King Edward I* was drafted to 88A Cardiff (Canton) in October 1961 and after withdrawal from there in June 1962 it had completed 1,570,015 miles. Since then it has been restored to traffic at Quainton Road. (D.K.Jones)

4) SR Rebuilt West *Country* Class 4-6-2 No 34008 *Padstow* a resident of 75A Brighton since August 1958, stands in the yard of its home shed on 2nd April 1961. Constructed at Eastleigh Works in September 1945, *Padstow* had been rebuilt during July 1960. From August 1962 it was no longer required by the operating authorities at Brighton and it was transferred to 71A Eastleigh. The final home for *Padstow* was at 70A Nine Elms, withdrawn in June 1967. (D.K.Jones)

5) A phalanx of upper quadrant signals occupy a large raised gantry in the background at Wood Green on 19th April 1961. Almost at the start of its northbound journey from Kings Cross is 1946 built Thompson LNER A2/3 Class 4-6-2 No 60514 *Chamossaire*, from 34E New England, which is in charge of an empty stock working. Like many a fine locomotive, *Chamossaire* was destined to be one of thousands withdrawn in 1962, in December in the case of No 60514. (T.R.Amos)

36) A panoramic view of Manchester (Central) with the domed roof dominating the background on 19th March 1961. We can just make out an unidentified LMS Class 4 2-6-4T standing bunker-first in the left of the frame whilst in the centre of the picture sister engine No 42596, of 27F Brunswick (Liverpool), sets off for home with a westbound express. On the right is one of the members of the 'Peak' Class main line diesels in charge of an express. (N.E.Preedy)

37) As steam was being run-down at 30A Stratford during the early sixties, the external care went to the wall as can be seen with the uncared for appearance of these two tank locomotives on 17th March 1961. Former Great Eastern Railway J67 Class 0-6-0T No 68565 shunts an unidentified LNER N7 Class 0-6-2T into a siding at Stratford shed. Once of 32C Lowestoft (Central), No 68565 joined the shed at 30A in November 1959. Withdrawal came in August 1962. (N.E.Preedy)

88) More tank engine power on show in London. This time the setting is the large complex (but nowhere near as large as Stratford) at 70A Nine Elms on the Southern Region. Occupying a section of the track in front of the straight running shed is Billinton designed former LBSCR E4 Class 0-6-2T No 32557 on 11th November 1961 shortly after being transferred to 70A from 73B Bricklayers Arms. It was condemned from 70A during December 1962. (N.L.Browne)

89) 34E New England based BR Class 9F 2-10-0 No 92038 trundles along the East Coast Main Line near to Hatfield with an up ballast train on Saturday 15th April 1961. This locomotive remained on the books at New England until June 1963 when it was reallocated to 40B Immingham. Just over twelve months later it returned to 34E but was drafted away again to 41J Langwith Junction in January 1965 from whence it was withdrawn three months later. (A.C.Ingram)

40) Two LNER L1 Class 2-6-4 Tanks are in harness at 52A Gateshead in September 1961 in the company of an unidentified LNER V2 Class 2-6-2. Both Nos 67742 and 67777 are allocated to 51A Darlington and during December 1961 they were transferred to 56B Ardsley in Leeds. All of the remaining members of the L1 Class were taken out of service by the end of 1962 and Nos 67742/77 survived until the end. Scrapping came at Darlington. (D.K.Jones)

41) Two 'foreigners' stand side to side outside the running shed at 67A Corkerhill (Glasgow) in the summer of 1961. On the left is a far from home 21A Saltley based LMS Rebuilt *Patriot*, Class 4-6-0 No 45532 *Illustrious* and on the right is BR *Britannia* Class 4-6-2 No 70054 *Dornoch Firth*, from 55A Leeds (Holbeck). Both of these engines ended their days in Carlisle No 45532 at 12B Upperby and No 70054 at 12A Kingmoor. (A.Rankin)

2) A less than clean 85B Gloucester (Horton Road) *Castle* Class 4-6-0 No 5071 *Spitfire*, heads the four coach portion of a Paddington to Hereford express through Malvern Wells on an undesignated date in 1961. Constructed during 1938 *Spitfire* was originally named *Clifford Castle* (which later became No 5098).The final home for *Spitfire* was at 82B St.Philip's Marsh and it was taken out of revenue earning traffic from there in October 1963. (Tim Farebrother)

3) A member of the station staff at Salisbury is engaged in conversation with the footplate crew of a Bulleid Light Pacific as other members of the railway fraternity fuss about on the platform under the watchful gaze of a lady passenger on 17th September 1961. The locomotive on view is SR Rebuilt *Battle of Britain* Class 4-6-2 No 34052 *Lord Dowding*, based at the local shed of 72B. It was eventually withdrawn from there in July 1967. (B.K.B.Green)

44) The final member (numerically speaking) of the BR Class 9F 2-10-0's No 92250, allocated to 86A Newport (Ebbw Junction), steams towards the camera as it departs from Gloucester and passes Over Junction with a Class 8 freight bound for South Wales on 17th March 1962. Released from Crewe Works in December 1958 (to 84C Banbury), No 92250 was equipped with a Giesl oblong ejector during 1959. This did little to prolong its life and it was condemned in December 1965. (N.E.Preedy)

5) Row upon row of gloomy tenement dwellings overlook the railway shed at 64A St.Margarets (Glasgow) on a wet and dismal 12th June 1962. On show in the yard is a begrimed LNER A2/3 Class 4-6-2 No 60519 *Honeyway*. Once based at the 'Top Link' depot at 64B Haymarket, *Honeyway* (built at Doncaster in February 1947) had been ousted from there by the encroaching diesel power and drafted to 64A in October 1961. It was withdrawn in December 1962. (F.Hornby)

6) Journey's end for an up express as it approaches the buffer stops at the mighty former Great Western Railway terminus at Paddington. GWR *Castle* Class 4-6-0 No 5054 *Earl of Ducie*. from 87G Carmarthen, eases itself past the photographer with an express from South Wales on 15th June 1962. *Earl of Ducie*, paired with a straight-sided tender, departed from South Wales for good in November 1963 when it was transferred to 86C Hereford. (D.K.Jones)

47) A line-up of locomotives are in steam together by the coal stage at 71A Eastleigh on an overcast day on 11th February 1962. From left to right they are:- SR W Class 2-6-4T No 31911, BR Class 3 2-6-2T No 82016, SR *Schools* Class 4-4-0 No 30934 *St.Lawrence* (70D Basingstoke) and BR Class 4 2-6-0 No 76006. Of these four engines, all were destined to die between December 1962 and July 1967, No 76006 being the last to succumb. (R.Picton)

48) Pacific power on show outside the small four-road former Caledonian Railway shed at 65J Stirling on 18th June 1962. LMS *Coronation* Class 4-6-2 No 46247 *City of Liverpool*, from 12A Carlisle (Kingmoor), is rostered to take charge of a Stirling to Sutton Coldfield car-sleeper duty which it will take as far as Carlisle. Accompanying *City of Liverpool* at Stirling shed is LMS Class 5 4-6-0 No 44959, allocated to 63A Perth. (F.Hornby)

9) Based largely on Sir Willian Stanier's Class 5 of LMS days, the BR Standard Class 5 4-6-0's totalled 172 in number. Constructed at Derby Works in December 1953 at a cost of £19,974, No 73049, from 82E Bristol Barrow Road, heads northwards through Defford, near Cheltenham, in June 1962 with a summer Saturday extra, M254. The last two homes for No 73049 were at 82F Bath Green Park and 81F Oxford. It was withdrawn from the latter in March 1965. (Tim Farebrother)

0) Two GWR *Castle* Class 4-6-0's monopolise the westbound tracks at Newport (High Street) on 24th April 1962. Halted at signals is No 5016 *Montgomery Castle* (87F Llanelly) with a relief express bound for Swansea. No 5016, equipped with a double chimney in January 1961, was withdrawn five months after this picture was taken. Steaming towards the camera on a centre road is No 7016 *Chester Castle*, from 88A Cardiff (Canton) with a milk train. (R.Picton)

51) A section of the compact water tank at Stockton-on-Tees station is occupied by an advertising hoarding as Gresley inspired LNER V2 Class 2-6-2 No 60847 *St.Peter's School, York AD 627*, from 50A York, pauses beneath the soot-stained overall roof to take on fresh water supplies. No 60847 is in charge of the 1.00pm cross-country express to Colchester on an unknown day in February 1962. It was withdrawn from York shed in June 1965. (G.D.Appleyard)

52) 1962 was the last year of operation for the surviving LMS *Princess* Class 4-6-2's and they were often employed on expresses and freight trains between England and Scotland. The pioneer member of the class, No 46200 *The Princess Royal*, based at 12A Carlisle (Kingmoor), takes a breather outside 65J Stirling shed on 18th August 1962, three months prior to withdrawal. In front of No 46200 is LMS Class 5 4-6-0 No 45357, a local steed. (J.Schatz)

3) A trio of GWR *Grange* Class 4-6-0's await their next duties on a road adjacent to the running shed at 83G Penzance on 15th April 1962. Nearest the camera is No 6835 *Estevarney Grange*, one of seventeen *Granges* allocated to 83G on this date. Within the next five months not only were all the *Granges* transferred away, but the depot had closed to steam. No 6835 went to 84B Oxley (Wolverhampton) during late April 1962. (N.E.Preedy)

4) The inhabitants of the dwellings in the background could hardly find a worse location to hang their washing than that of the busy junction at Clapham, especially if the wind was in the wrong direction. Black smoke is issued from the funnel of SR *Merchant Navy* Class 4-6-2 No 35014 *Nederland Line*, from 70A Nine Elms, as it speeds by with the down *Atlantic Coast Express* from Waterloo on 4th August 1962. (F.Hornby)

55) LMS *Jubilee* Class 4-6-0 No 45585 *Hyderabad* looks in dire need of the attentions of the cleaning staff at 17A Derby as it passes Mangotsfield station (closed in 1966) on the outskirts of Bristol on 17th March 1962, light engine. Between January 1957 and withdrawal in May 1964, *Hyderabad* was based at a variety of sheds, Derby (twice), Kentish Town (twice), Neasden, Leicester Midland (twice), Newton Heath and Burton-on-Trent. (D.K.Jones)

56) BR *Britannia* Class 4-6-2 No 70046 *Anzac* was the last member of the class to be named, in September 1959, leaving No 70047 as the only example never to carry a name. On 6th May 1962 No 70046 is seen at its new abode of 21D Aston fresh from a transfer from 1A Willesden. It was destined to remain at Aston until December 1962, moving to 6J Holyhead. Behind *Anzac* is an unidentified LMS Class 5 4-6-0. On the left is LMS *Jubilee* Class 4-6-0 No 45684 *Jutland*. (N.E.Preedy)

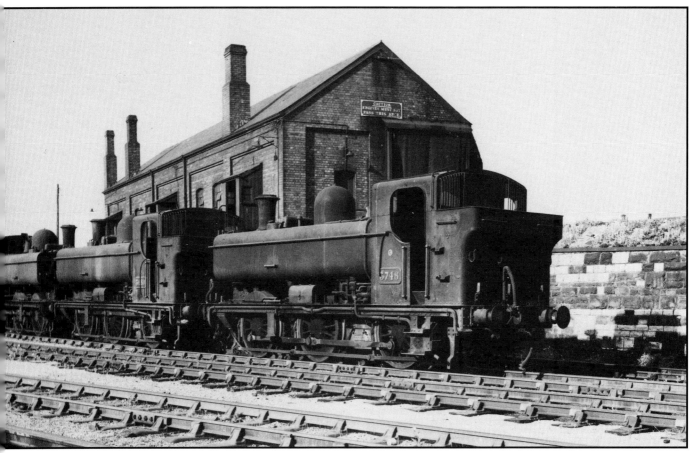

57) A trio of former Great Western Railway 0-6-0 Pannier Tanks are lined up in front of the imposing brick-built coaling plant at 88C Barry on a sun-filled 12th September 1962. Nearest the camera is No 3748, a resident of Barry since a move from 88A Cardiff (Canton) the previous month. Prior to moving to South Wales in September 1961, No 3748 had a lengthy spell at Bristol, being based at both 82A Bath Road and 82B St.Philip's Marsh. (D.K.Jones)

58) Hordes of trainspotters occupy the platforms at Eastleigh station on 1st August 1962 during the main school holidays. All will make a note of the passing of SR U Class 2-6-0 No 31619, from the nearby shed at 71A, as it coasts along light engine in what appears to be ex. works condition. A longstanding resident of 71A, No 31619 moved on to pastures new at 75C Norwood Junction in November 1962. It ended its days from 70C Guildford in December 1965. (N.L.Browne)

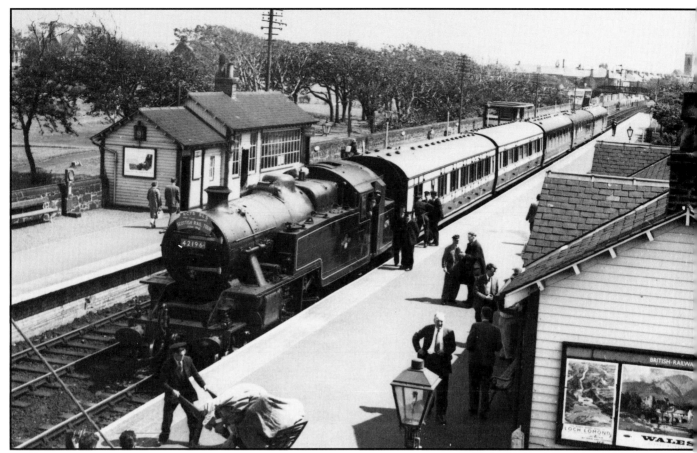

59) A perfect summer's day at Ardrossan South Beach station on 22nd June 1962. As some members of the railway staff go about their business, a spruced-up LMS Class 4 2-6-4T No 42196, of 67C Ayr (withdrawn in May 1967), pauses with a joint RCTS/SLS railtour, the stock of which includes two former Caledonian coaches. At its height Ardrossan boasted no less than five stations:- Harbour, Montgomerie Pier, North, South Beach and Town. (N.E.Preedy)

60) BR Class 4 4-6-0 No 75073, from 82F Bath Green Park, accelerates away from Midford station amidst a sylvan setting on 1st September 1962, shortly before the end of the summer timetable. No 75073, fitted with a double chimney, is in charge of a three-coach passenger service from Bath to Templecombe. Once of 71A Eastleigh, No 75073 had been on the former S & D since February 1957 and it remained there until withdrawal in December 1965. (N.E.Preedy)

51) 1962 was an infamous year with regards to the wholesale slaughter of steam engines. Many classes were rendered extinct and others suffered from large scale condemnations. On view on a side track at 62C Dunfermline are two doomed locomotives from two of the classes which disappeared during 1962. On the left is former NBR J88 Class 0-6-0T No 68346 and on the right is another ex. NBR example, Y9 Class 0-4-0ST No 68101, photographed in June 1962. (F.Hornby)

52) Prior to 1962, the fourteen members of the SR USA Class 0-6-0 Tanks had been unaffected by withdrawals, but by the end of 1962 their numbers had been reduced to eight in the normal sense of the word. Only one was actually scrapped, No 30063, as the others, Nos 30061/62/65/ 66/70 were taken into Departmental stock. On 25th March 1962, No 30072, based at the local docks shed (71I), is photographed in steam in Southampton New Docks. (W.Boyden)

CHAPTER FOUR - 1963

63) A 'fed-up' looking railwayman leans against a grubby lampost in the shed yard at 82E Bristol (Barrow Road) on 24th August 1963. In steam behind him are an unidentified LMS Class 8F 2-8-0, LMS *Jubilee* Class 4-6-0 No 45668 *Madden*, from 17B Burton, and BR Class 5 4-6-0 No 73028, a local steed. Whilst the latter had in excess of three years to live, withdrawal was on the horizon for *Madden* which was condemned in December 1963 from Burton. (T.Nicholls)

54) Once of 73A Stewarts Lane (until June 1959) SR *Merchant Navy* Class 4-6-2 No 35028 *Clan Line* drifts slowly out of Waterloo station and heads for its home base at 70A Nine Elms after bringing in an express from the west on 9th August 1963. Constructed at Eastleigh Works in December 1948, *Clan Line* was rebuilt in October 1959. After withdrawal from Nine Elms at the end of Southern steam in July 1967 it was preserved by the Merchant Navy Loco Society. (N.E.Preedy)

55) We move from the English capital to the centre of Scotland, where, on a soaking wet day in March 1963 we espy an immaculate BR Class 2 2-6-0 No 78052 outside the straight running shed at 63A Perth, a depot it had been based at since July 1962. Other sheds from which No 78052 was allocated in Scotland were at:- 60A Inverness, 60B Aviemore and 64F Bathgate. It was condemned from the latter in January 1966 and scrapped at Motherwell. (R.Butterfield)

66) The world steam record holder, LNER A4 Class 4-6-2 No 60022 *Mallard* (34A Kings Cross) finds itself on alien territory during a photo-stop at Tiverton Junction on the Western Region with the Paddington bound leg of an enthusiasts special on 24th February 1963, having been serviced at Exmouth Junction shed in Exeter. Two months on and *Mallard* was no longer with us in the normal sense though it was preserved for posterity by British Railways. (G.H.Truran)

67) GWR 5600 Class 0-6-2T No 6688, from 86G Pontypool Road, departs from Hafodyrynys Tunnel in a flurry of steam as it nears Crumlin with a Neath to Pontypool road local passenger service on 10th October 1963. Until June 1961, when the shed closed to steam, No 6688 was an inhabitant of 87E Landore (Swansea). It then moved the short distance to 87D Swansea East Dock. Its last abode was at 88F Treherbert from whence it was withdrawn in April 1964. (W.Potter)

58) This photograph epitomizes the way things used to be in motive power depots in years gone by, with the yard packed with steam locomotives. Amongst the engines on view at 55D Royston on a sunny 21st July 1963 are BR Class 5 4-6-0's Nos 73166 and 73171 , LMS Class 8F 2-8-0's Nos 48080 and 48473 and WD Class 8F 2-8-0 No 90605. This former LMS shed, coded 20C from 1948 to 1957, was closed to steam by the NER authorities on 6th November 1967. (T.R.Amos)

59) A less than well maintained SR Q Class 0-6-0 No 30545, from 75E Three Bridges, is probably in for overhaul at the nearby workshops as it stands in the yard at 71A Eastleigh on 23rd June 1963. No 30545 is hemmed between an ex.works SR *Merchant Navy* Class 4-6-2 and a BR Class 4 2-6-0. Once based at 75D Horsham, No 30545 had moved to Three Bridges in July 1959. Its final home was at 70A Nine Elms where it was to die in April 1965. (T.R.Amos)

70) Once a proud member of the small fleet of BR *Britannia* Class 4-6-2's based on the Western Region at Cardiff (Canton) shed, No 70029 *Shooting Star* found itself on the London Midland Region by September 1961 at 21D Aston. On 1st September 1963 it was still at 21D and is noted on a heavily laden morning express from Euston to Blackpool, at Rugby (Midland). It remained at Aston shed until October 1964 when it was drafted north to 12A Carlisle (Kingmoor). (D.K.Jones)

71) With the large wooden coaling stage dominating the background LNER V2 Class 2-6-2 No 60804, allocated to 62B Dundee Tay Eridge, gently lifts its safety valves at the former Caledonian Railway depot at 65B St.Rollox in Glasgow. Judging by the fine external condition it is fresh from overhaul on 10th April 1963. No 60804 survived in service until December 1963. (N.E.Preedy)

2) Having not long changed codes from 84E to 2A, Tyseley based GWR *Hall* Class 4-6-0 No 6930 *Aldersey Hall* displays its new shedcode on its smokebox as it rests near to the coaling plant at Tyseley on 24th September 1963. From January 1957 until withdrawal in October 1965, *Aldersey Hall* was allocated to 85A Worcester, 84F Stourbridge, 84A Wolverhampton (Stafford Road) and 2D Banbury. It was cut up on site at Banbury in February 1966. (W.Wood)

3) LMS *Jubilee* Class 4-6-0 No 45690 *Leander* (82E Bristol Barrow Road) is primed and ready for action as it stands by a colour light signal on a centre road at Bristol (Temple Meads) station on 7th September 1963 a few short months before withdrawal in March 1964 from 82E. *Leander* is rostered to take over a northbound express to Birmingham and beyond. Preserved by the Leander Loco Society in May 1972 it has since been active on main line expresses. (B.J.Ashworth)

74) Rubbish of all descriptions is piled high on the loading deck near to the small goods yard at Evesham on 1st June 1963. The peace and quiet of the small station is disturbed momentarily as GWR 5700 Class 0-6-0PT No 4614, of 85B Gloucester (Horton Road), bustles away bunker-first with the lightly loaded 3.41pm Saturdays Only local passenger to Ashchurch. After withdrawal from 85B in July 1964, No 4614 was cut up at Birds, Morriston. (J.M.Tolson)

75) A quartet of steam locomotives and a diesel 0-6-0 shunter occupy tracks in front of the straight running shed at 75C Norwood Junction on 26th May 1963. Three of the steam engines can be identified as SR U Class 2-6-0 No 31807, SR W Class 2-6-4T No 31919 and N Class 2-6-0 No 31827 a visitor to 75C from 75B Redhill. The depot, of Southern Railway origin, closed to steam on 6th January 1964. Most of its allocation was transferred to other depots. (T.R.Amos)

6) By early July 1963 the dump at 64F Bathgate was well established and steam locomotives from many parts of Scotland were to be noted in row after row of forlorn dereliction, some still with their tenders well stocked with coal. In this picture there is a line-up of four LNER V2 Class 2-6-2's with No 60819, withdrawn from 64A St.Margarets (Edinburgh) at the forefront. Bringing up the rear is former NBR D34 Class 4-4-0 No 62484 *Glen Lyon*. (J.Wraithmell)

7) A deserted platform at Barmouth on the Welsh coast on a dismal 12th June 1963. In charge of the 3.45pm local passenger, train to Portmadoc, consisting of just three carriages. is BR Class 4 4-6-0 No 75002, from 89C Machynlleth. From January 1957 until January 1960, No 75002 was based at 82C Swindon. Later in its career it served at 85E Gloucester (Barnwood), 82G Templecombe, 82E Bristol Barrow Road, 6C Croes Newydd and 5D Stoke. (F.Hornby)

78) 86G Pontypool Road based GWR 5101 Class 2-6-2T No 4157 looks in fine fettle outside the shed at 85B Gloucester (Horton Road) in company with an unidentified GWR 2800 Class 2-8-0. Peeping out of the shed is a visitor from 84E Tyseley, GWR *Modified Hall* Class 4-6-0 No 6971 *Athelhampton Hall*, which was destined to die there in October 1964. No 4157 fared a little better, lingering on until June 1965 at 86E Severn Tunnel Junction. (D.K.Jones)

79) Numerous steam locomotives are scattered around the shed yard at 70A Nine Elms on 4th May 1963. In the distance are two GWR 5700 Class 0-6-0 Pannier Tanks. Nearer the camera (left) is BR Class 3 2-6-2T No 82019 and a SR Unrebuilt Light Pacific. In the centre of the frame is BR Class 3 2-6-2T No 82024 in ex. works condition. This latter engine had been a longstanding resident of 72A Exmouth Junction until moving to Nine Elms in October 1962. (N.L.Browne)

0) The railway scene at Lancaster as seen from an obtuse angle on 15th July 1963. A screen of smoke and steam combine to partially obscure LMS Class 5 4-6-0 No 45083, from 27C Southport, as it passes the No. 3 signalbox with an unidentified express. For many years a Carlisle engine at both 12A Kingmoor and 12B Upperby sheds, No 45083 had been at Southport depot since May 1963. In June 1964 it was drafted to 9D Newton Heath (Manchester). (D.K.Jones)

1) Possibly carrying the shortest name of any locomotive on British Railways, LNER Bl Class 4-6-0 No 61018 *Gnu*, allocated to 50A York, stands at Malton with a rake of coaches on a misty 1st October 1963. Prior to being based at York from September 1960 until condemnation in November 1965, *Gnu* was allocated to 51E Stockton, 51G Haverton Hill, 51L Thornaby, 51A Darlington and 56A Wakefield. It was cut up at Drapers, Hull in February 1966. (N.E.Preedy)

82) Constructed at the height of the Second World War, in June 1942, SR Rebuilt *Merchant Navy* Class 4-6-2 No 35007 *Aberdeen Commonwealth*, from 70G Weymouth, finds itself many miles from home at York on11th December 1964. It is seen here on York shed (50A) with steam to spare. *Aberdeen Commonwealth*, once a longstanding resident of Salisbury depot, is being employed by the Warwickshire Railway Society on a special to and from Birmingham. (N.E.Preedy)

3) GWR *Castle* Class 4-6-0 No 7025 *Sudeley Castle* stands in the yard of its home shed at 85A Worcester in the spring of 1964. Next to *Sudeley Castle* is sister locomotive No 7034 *Ince Castle*, a visitor to the depot from 85B Gloucester (Horton Road). Built at Swindon Works, *Sudeley Castle* was withdrawn in September 1964 after a life of only fifteen years. *Ince Castle* followed suit in June 1965 from 85B. Both engines were cut up in South Wales. (Tim Farebrother)

4) Despite being a favourite amongst the allocation of steam locomotives to 62B Dundee Tay Bridge, BR Class 4 2-6-4T No 80124 has been somewhat neglected by the cleaners at the depot on 6th July 1964. Standing by a soot-stained wall at Tay Bridge station, No 80124 is ready for departure with the 12.28 local passenger to Tayport. In February 1966 it was drafted to 64A St.Margarets (Edinburgh) but was condemned from there ten months later. (A.F.Nisbet)

85) Unlike No 80124 in the previous picture SR Unrebuilt *Battle of Britain* Class 4-6-2 No 34064 *Fighter Command* (equipped with a Giesl Oblong Ejector in May 1962) looks in pristine condition in the yard at 70A Nine Elms in May 1964. Allocated to 70D Eastleigh, *Fighter Command* is ready for its next duty. Despite having the advantage of the Giesl Oblong Ejector to save on fuel consumption it did not prolong the life of No 34064, which was withdrawn in May 1966. (A.C.Ingram)

86) Another Pacific looking in fine external fettle is LNER A4 Class 4-6-2 No 60004 *William Whitelaw*, as photographed in the almost deserted depot yard at 65B St.Rollox in Glasgow in July 1964. *William Whitelaw* is a visitor to 65B from 61B Aberdeen (Ferryhill). Ousted by diesel power from 64B Haymarket in June 1962 it returned there three months later, but was ousted again on a permanent basis in July 1963. Withdrawal came in July 1966. (A.C.Ingram)

7) The copse in the background is laden with foliage as BR Class 5 4-6-0 No 73075, from 66A Polmadie (Glasgow), coasts along with a fitted freight at Floriston on the borders of England and Scotland between Carlisle and Gretna on 1st August 1964. Situated on the West Coast Main Line, Floriston at one time boasted a station and a set of water troughs. Both are long gone as is No 73075, withdrawn from Polmadie shed in December 1965. (D.K.Jones)

8) We move from the West Coast Main Line to the former Midland Main Line as LMS Class 8F 2-8-0 No 48356, of 15B Wellingborough, approaches Kegworth station in a flurry of steam at the head of a northbound mixed freight train on 6th April 1964. In July 1965, No 48356 was transferred to the Manchester area, being initially based at 9E Trafford Park. It later served at 9F Heaton Mersey and 9D Newton Heath before condemnation in June 1968. (K.L.Seal)

89) By autumn 1963 the former Southern Railway lines and depots in Devon and Cornwall became the property of the Western Region and it was only a matter of time before Southern steam was to be wiped out. In this photograph SR Unrebuilt *Battle of Britain* Class 4-6-2 No 34054 *Lord Beaverbrook* has been smartly turned out by the shed staff at Exmouth Junction as it stands at Exeter Central station on 2nd August 1964 ten months before the end of steam in the area. (D.Webster)

90) After what was probably its last major overhaul GWR 6100 Class 2-6-2T No 6147, from 85A Worcester, looks resplendent in lined green livery outside 'A' shop at Swindon Works on 26th April 1964. Introduced in January 1933 for duties on the London surburban services, it was initially shedded at Southall depot. By November 1960 it was to be found in the Bristol area at 82B St.Philip's Marsh. It was withdrawn in December 1965. (Tim Farebrother)

91) Despite the ever growing legions of diesels being introduced into the north-east of England some steam survivors still put in appearances at the once mighty depot at Gateshead which is situated by the River Tyne on the outskirts of Newcastle. 50A York based LNER A1 Class 4-6-2 No 60121 *Silurian* is a visitor to 52A on 24th October 1964 as rests between duties outside the 'Pacific Shed'. By October 1965 *Silurian* was with us no more. (H.L.Holland)

92) A crowded scene 'beneath the wires' at Glasgow (Central) on an unknown September day in 1964. By this stage in time the majority of workings were either diesel hauled or in the hands of electric multiple units. One exception were the workings to and from Greenock and Gourock. A begrimed LMS Class 4 2-6-4T No 42264, from 66D Greenock, sets off from Central with such a train. No 42264 lasted at Greenock shed until July 1966. (A.Rankin)

93) Four BR Standard types of locomotives are visible in this picture taken at 70A Nine Elms in May 1964. In the left of the frame we can identify BR Class 3 2-6-2T No 82015. Taking centre stage is BR Class 5 4-6-0 No 73087 *Linette*. Both engines are native to 70A. No 73087, adopted the name of *Linette* from SR *King Arthur* Class 4-6-0 No 30752 several years after the latter was withdrawn. No 73087 survived in service until October 1966. (A.C.Ingram)

94) A soaking wet day at Penrith station on 6th June 1964 on the West Coast Main Line. This is the unlikely setting for 56B Ardsley based LNER V2 Class 2-6-2 No 60923 which is in charge of the Locomotive Club of Great Britain inspired 'North Countryman' Railtour. Allocated to 52A Gateshead for many years, No 60923 was drafted to Ardsley in December 1962. It had been fitted with outside steampipes in February 1957, some eight years prior to withdrawal. (D.Webster)

95) Looking fresh from overhaul GWR *Modified Hall* Class 4-6-0 No 7928 *Wolf Hall*, with a well stocked tender, stands in a platform at Gloucester (Central) with a stopping passenger train on 6th March 1964. Constructed at Swindon Works by British Railways, *Wolf Hall* spent most of its short working life allocated to 85A Worcester. Condemnation came in March 1965 and it was despatched to its graveyard at its birthplace the following month. (R.W.Hinton)

96) Two mixed traffic Class 5 locomotives of different design and origins stand close to one another in the shed yard at 64C Dalry Road (Edinburgh) on a summer Sunday in 1964. Nearest the camera is Stanier LMS 4-6-0 No 45011, from 66E Carstairs. In the right of the frame is Thompson B1 4-6-0 No 61351, a local engine which is in store. On a visit to Dalry Road on 4th August 1964 by the author there were just ten steam locomotives to be seen. (A.Rankin)

97) Despite its fine external condition SR Unrebuilt *West Country* Class 4-6-2 No 34107 *Blandford Forum* was just one month or so away from withdrawal from 83D Exmouth Junction when this photograph was taken on 30th August 1964. *Blandford Forum* is parked adjacent to the compact wooden signalbox at Axminster as it heads a Waterloo to Exeter Central express. After withdrawal it was stored briefly then despatched to Birds, Morriston for scrapping. (A.Jones)

98) A few months before being taken out of revenue earning service from 81C Southall in December 1964, a bedraggled looking Churchward GWR 2800 Class 2-8-0 No 2873 replenishes its tender at Malvern Wells station prior to attacking the gradient to Colwall tunnel with a lengthy freight. Built in 1918, No 2873 later served at a variety of depots, including 86E Severn Tunnel Junction and 86J/88J Aberdare. Today, it is in the hands of the preservationists. (Tim Farebrother)

9) Shorn of nameplates and shedplate a mighty Pacific has been steamed for the last time and it awaits its inevitable fate at 64A St.Margarets (Edinburgh) in October 1964. Once the pride of 52B Heaton, LNER A3 Class 4-6-2 No 60077 *The White Knight* had been condemned three months earlier from 64A. Apart from serving at Heaton shed, *The White Knight* was also based at Leeds (Holbeck), Copley Hill and Ardsley sheds before moving to Scotland in July 1963. (A.Rankin)

00) As former Great Western types vanished from the railway scene the remaining spaces for steam repairs at Swindon Works were rapidly filled by locomotives from other regions. Here we see a typical example, in the shape of Stanier LMS Class 6P5F 2-6-0 No 42945, from 5E Nuneaton, which is seen minus its tender outside 'A' shop on 29th November 1964. During the following month, No 42945 was reallocated to 9G Gorton in Manchester. (N.L.Browne)

101) The last rostered steam hauled express from Paddington during 1965 was the 4.15pm to Banbury. On 26th March 1965 we observe the footplate crew of begrimed GWR *Modified Hall* Class 4-6-0 No 6983 *Otterington Hall*, of 81E Didcot, looking towards the rear of the train as it stands in Platform Three. When Didcot shed closed in June 1965, *Otterington Hall* was drafted to 81F Oxford. Its stay of execution was only brief and it was withdrawn two months later. (J.Schatz)

02) Sunlight and shadow at 6G Llandudno Junction in June 1965. LMS Class 5 4-6-0 No 45345, from 6J Holyhead, is noted at rest between the turntable, water tower and the running shed. Between January 1957 and May 1967, No 45345 was based at depots on the North Wales Main Line. Apart from 6J Holyhead it was at 6H Bangor, 6G Llandudno Junction and 6A Chester. Its final abode was at 10D Lostock Hall, being condemned from there in June 1968. (N.L.Browne)

03) One of the last surviving Gresley LNER A3 Class 4-6-2's No 60052 *Prince Palatine*, based at 64A St.Margarets (Edinburgh), has been spruced up on 5th June 1965 to haul a special and is seen at Carlisle (Citadel) station. For many years it was a North Eastern Region engine until moving to 64A in September 1963. After withdrawal from St.Margarets in January 1966 it lay in store for six months before being despatched to Langloan for scrapping. (D.Webster)

104) A phalanx of somewhat 'overloaded' telegraph posts and wires stretch into infinity at Worting Junction, near Basingstoke, on the former London and South Western Railway Main Line from Waterloo. Approaching the camera at speed is SR Rebuilt *Merchant Navy* Class 4-6-2 No 35023 *Holland-Afrika Line* (70F Bournemouth) with an express on 3rd April 1965. Destined to survive until the end of steam in July 1967, No 35023 was withdrawn from 70A Nine Elms. (Ken Ellis)

105) On an unknown day in the summer of 1965, 2A Tyseley based GWR *Modified Hall* Class 4-6-0 No 7915 *Mere Hall*, stripped of nameplates, finds employment at Birmingham (Snow Hill) as the station pilot. At this stage in time there were just three *Modified Halls* left on the books at Tyseley shed, the other two being Nos 7908 *Henshall Hall* and 7929 *Wyke Hall*. By October of this same year all three were a memory in the Birmingham area. (D.K.Jones)

06) A crowded section of the huge shed yard at 50A York on 10th July 1965. Lined up in the sunshine from left to right are: LMS Class 4 'Flying Pig' 2-6-0 No 43078, from 50B Hull (Dairycoates), an unidentified BR Class 9F 2-10-0, LNER V2 Class 2-6-2 No 60831, a local inhabitant, and LMS Class 5 4-6-0 No 44854, from 55A Leeds (Holbeck). York shed once boasted a host of V2 2-6-2's but by mid-1965 they were in their death throes. (N.E.Preedy)

07) A rain-soaked and miserable looking day at 82F Bath Green Park on 12th June 1965. In the foreground we espy a local steed in the shape of BR Class 5 4-6-0 No 73054, one of a small batch of the same allocated to 82F. In front of No 73054 is a converted tender off an unknown locomotive. Once of 17A Derby and 22A/82E Bristol Barrow Road, No 73054 had been at Bath Green Park since April 1961. It was to die there during August 1965. (D.K.Jones)

108) Neglect has taken its toll over the years with GWR *Manor* Class 4-6-0 No 7816 *Frilsham Manor*, as can be seen by the letters 'G.W.R.' which has emerged on the tender through what must have been a layer of 'British Railways' paint! *Frilsham Manor* is noted in steam in the yard of its home shed at 81E Didcot on 26th April 1965. Despite being closed in June 1965, today, Didcot is a thriving centre of the preservation movement. (D.K.Jones)

109) LMS Ivatt Class 2 2-6-2T No 41312 stands adjacent to its abode at 70F Bournemouth in March 1965 amidst bright sunshine with some coaching stock. No 41312 spent all of its working life on the Southern Region and in its latter years it was to be found at 73E Faversham, 73F Ashford, 72E Barnstaple Junction, 75A Brighton and 70A Nine Elms (as well as 70F Bournemouth). It was condemned from Nine Elms shed during July 1967. (R.Butterfield)

10) The driver of BR Class 4 4-6-0 No 75004, from 6F Machynlleth, fitted with a double chimney but minus shedplate, looks forward towards the photographer as his charge lets off steam in Portmadoc station. No 75004 is heading a local passenger train on 18th October 1965. Apart from being allocated to Machynlleth shed, No 75004 also served from a variety of depots in the twilight of its career, including 86C Cardiff (Canton). (N.E.Preedy)

11) Although taken out of normal revenue earning service from 71I Southampton Docks in October 1962, SR USA Class 0-6-0T No 30070 was immediately taken in Departmental Stock which lengthened its life on BR for almost a further five years. It was renumbered DS238 and named *Wainwright* and posted to Ashford Works in its new guise. It is seen as Eastleigh Works sporting a fresh coat of paint in August 1965. It is now preserved on the Kent & East Sussex Railway. (N.E.Preedy)

112) A splendid panoramic view of Carstairs shed and station on 3rd June 1965. In the foreground is an unidentified LMS Class 5 4-6-0. Note the carriage sidings in the left of the frame and the concrete coaling plant in the background. By this date in time the allocation at this former Caledonian Railway depot had dwindled somewhat. On the occasion of the author's last visit, in August 1964, twenty-three steam locomotives were noted. (D.Webster)

113) Another panoramic view, this time on the Southern main line at Basingstoke in the summer of 1965, looking towards the direction of London. Heading towards the signal gantry is an unidentified SR *Merchant Navy* Class 4-6-2 with an express bound for Southampton and beyond. In the right of the picture is 70E Salisbury based SR Unrebuilt *Battle of Britain* Class 4-6-2 No 34051 *Winston Churchill*, which is in charge of a westbound express. (John Smith)

14) In common with a host of major stations Leicester (Midland) had extensive carriage sidings within close proximity to the station. In July 1965 the sidings are quite full as locally based BR Class 3 2-6-0 No 78061 performs manouvres within the sidings. One of a numerical batch of the same, allocated at one time to 27D Wigan (L & Y) - Nos 78060-64, No 78061 had been at 15A Leicester (Midland) since September 1964. It ended its days at 16A Toton. (R.S.Carpenter)

15) Newly allocated to 51C West Hartlepool from 52K Consett, former North Eastern Railway Q6 Class 0-8-0 No 63368 (minus numberplate) is pressed into service with a train of coal empties at West Hartlepool on 28th May 1965. The locomotive looks in a rundown condition, as is the area of tracks and sidings over which it is proceeding. No 63368 was condemned from 51C in December 1966 and a few months later it was despatched to Drapers, Hull. (N.E.Preedy)

116) With steam to spare, begrimed BR Class 9F 2-10-0 No 92237 of 86B Newport (Ebbw Junction), powers its way along on quadruped track at Haresfield station, south of Gloucester, on the main line from Birmingham to Bristol, with a heavy southbound freight on 29th July 1965. Released into traffic in September 1958 to Ebbw Junction shed, No 92237 equipped with a double chimney, was less than two months away from withdrawal when photographed. (K.L.Seal)

117) On a sunny day on 10th May 1965, locally based GWR 6100 Class 2-6-2T No 6161 hauls a 'failed' Hymeck Type 3 Diesel-Hydraulic engine away from Southall station and heads for London and 81A Old Oak Common. Note that No 6161 has lost its side numberplates, being replaced by stencilled ones, a common practice for former GWR steam locomotives by 1965. It was drafted to 81F Oxford in September 1965, but withdrawn the following month. (D.K.Jones)

18) Although the motion is well greased and the tender is filled with coal supplies it is doubtful if British Railways built (1948) but LNER inspired Peppercorn Al Class 4-6-2 No 60138 *Boswell* ever turned a wheel in revenue earning service again. It is photographed at its home shed at 50A York in store with the mark of doom (a sacked chimney) on 10th September 1965. Officially condemned the following month it was cut up at Killamarsh. (D.K.Jones)

19) By February 1965 the steam allocation at the former South East and Chatham Railway shed at 75B Redhill had dwindled to a handful, including BR Class 4 2-6-4T No 80144, seen in steam by the compact running shed structure. Once of Neasden shed on the Eastern Region, No 80144 had moved to the Southern Region in November 1959 being initially allocated to 75A Brighton. After Redhill depot closed it moved west to 70E Salisbury. (A.C.Ingram)

120) With the fireman looking forwards from the cab of his charge, BR Class 5 4-6-0 No 73089 *Maid of Astolat,* from 70C Guildford, nears the end of its relatively short working life as it departs from Waterloo station with the 18.09 hours semi-fast passenger train for Basingstoke on 11th August 1966. Bearing in mind the dreadful external condition in which *Maid of Astolat* is seen, it is not surprising it was withdrawn the following month. (M.S.Stokes)

21) Beneath the wires at Elsecar Junction on former Great Central Railway territory near to Wath-on-Dearne on a misty 13th August 1966. The lengthy rake of coaches disappearing into the distance are occupied by the clientele of the Railway Correspondence and Travel Society inspired 'Great Central Railtour'. The motive power employed is LNER Bl Class 4-6-0 No 61131, of 56A Wakefield, which was taken out of service four months later. (N.E.Preedy)

22) Three separate regions of British Railways are represented in this photograph, with a North Eastern coach situated behind the tender of a London Midland engine on Southern metals. 2B Oxley based LMS Class 5 4-6-0 No 44856 charges out of Brockenhurst station with a holiday express on 1st July 1966. Within a year or so scenes like this were to become a memory on the Southern Region, as was No 44856, condemned in February 1967 from Oxley. (D.K.Jones)

123) Although stripped of its shedplate, 70E Salisbury based SR Rebuilt *Battle of Britain* Class 4-6-2 No 34056 *Croydon* still proudly carries its nameplates as it blows off excess steam at Basingstoke station beneath leaden skies on 15th October 1966. *Croydon* is in charge of a heavy down express from Waterloo to Weymouth. Prior to being allocated to Salisbury shed in October 1963, *Croydon* had been a longstanding inmate of 72A Exmouth Junction. (R.W.Hinton)

124) Bright winter sunshine enlivens the railway scene at Mirfield station on the North Eastern Region which is playing host to a light engine from 40B Immingham on the Eastern Region in the shape of LNER B1 Class 4-6-0 No 61250 *A.Harold Bibby*. This locomotive had been at Immingham shed since September 1963 having had spells at 36A Doncaster, 34E New England and 34F Grantham. It was withdrawn from revenue earning service in April 1966. (N.E.Preedy)

25) By mid 1966 steam was very much on the retreat in Scotland due to heavy withdrawals from 1962 onwards and mighty sheds like the one at Corkerhill in Glasgow were soon to lose their allocations. Still 'alive' on 15th July of this year is a less than clean BR Class 5 4-6-0 No 73120 which was destined to be doomed in December 1966. Peeping out of the running shed is sister locomotive No 73101 which was condemned a month after this picture was taken. (C.P.Stacey)

26) Another depot in its death throes with regards to the elimination of steam was at Saltley in Birmingham, coded 21A and 2E under British Railways, which closed to steam on 6th March 1967. Gathered inside a section of the 'open' roundhouse at Saltley on 17th September 1966 are three lifeless locomotives. From left to right they are:- BR Class 9F 2-10-0's Nos 92151 and 92150 along with LMS Stanier Class 8F 2-8-0 No 48220. (Mike Wood)

127) The 'honour' of being the last steam locomotive to be outshopped at Eastleigh Works fell to SR Rebuilt *Battle of Britain* Class 4-6-2 No 34089 *602 Squadron*, from 70E Salisbury, which departed from the works on 3rd October 1966, being recorded for posterity by the BBC childrens programme 'Blue Peter' (which in later years recorded the overhaul of LNER A2 Class 4-6-2 No 60532 *Blue Peter*). No 34089 is noted in the yard outside 70D Eastleigh in late October 1966. (D.K.Jones)

128) Bleak moorlands brood over the isolated Settle & Carlisle main line at Garsdale as LMS Class 5 4-6-0 No 44833, allocated to 5B Crewe (South), traverses a viaduct with a mixed freight on 28th May 1966. No 44833 spent many years at 2A Rugby before being transferred to 1A Willesden in June 1964. Twelve months later it was drafted to Crewe (South) which was to be its last abode until withdrawn in September 1967. (D.K.Jones)

29) With safety valves lifting gently, 12A Carlisle (Kingmoor) based BR Class 9F 2-10-0 No 92110 threads its way through ranks of goods trucks of all descriptions, including some 'door to door' containers, at Carnforth on 15th August 1966. From early 1957 until May 1965, when it moved to Kingmoor, No 92110 served at a variety of depots, these being:14A Cricklewood, 15A Wellingborough, 15C Leicester (Midland), 16E Kirkby and 9D Newton Heath. (D.K.Jones)

30) Once based in the far reaches of Norfolk, at 32A Norwich, LNER B1 Class 4-6-0 No 61042 is in a sorry state in the shed yard at 50A York on 17th February 1966 where it is a visitor from 36A Doncaster. After leaving Norwich in December 1959, No 61042 moved to 31B March. Two months later it was on the move again, this time to 40A Lincoln where it remained until September 1963. It was withdrawn from 36A during April 1966. (D.K.Jones)

131) The last depot to house the once numerous Hughes LMS Class 6P5F 'Crab' 2-6-0's was at Birkenhead, coded 6C and 8H under BR. One of their ranks, No 42765, is noted in steam in the depot yard on 6th June 1966 in the company of BR Class 9F 2-10-0 No 92113 a local engine, allocated here since July 1965. No 42765 had moved to Birkenhead from 24F/10C Fleetwood in April 1964. It was rendered redundant from the shed at the end of 1966. (R.Picton)

132) Another locomotive which was destined to die at the end of 1966 was BR Class 5 4-6-0 No 73080 *Merlin* (70G Weymouth) seen here emerging from a tunnel at Upwey, between Poole and Weymouth, with a passenger working on 30th July 1966. The name 'Merlin' was once carried by SR *King Arthur* Class 4-6-0 No 30740. During the late fifties No 73080 was based at 73A Stewarts Lane and 70A Nine Elms. It also served from 71A Eastleigh. (W.Piggott)

133) Another Weymouth locomotive finds itself on 'foreign' territory beneath the magnificent overall roof at York where watering facilities are adjacent to a colour light signal gantry. The visitor is SR *Merchant Navy* Class 4-6-2 No 35026 *Lamport & Holt Line* which is being employed on the AERS 'Elizabethan Railtour' on 20th November 1966. Constructed at Eastleigh Works in December 1948 it was withdrawn from 70G in March 1967. (N.E.Preedy)

134) Looking in ex. works condition BR Class 9F 2-10-0 No 92002, from 2A Tyseley, looks in refreshing external condition as it moves around the shed yard at 2D Banbury on 29th April 1966. One of a batch allocated to 86A Newport (Ebbw Junction) in the mid-fifties, Nos 92000-7, this engine departed from South Wales in May 1963. Ousted from the Midlands in December 1966 it moved to 8H Birkenhead from whence it was withdrawn in November 1967. (D.K.Jones)

135) Although looking in respectable external condition it is the end of the road for BR Class 4 2-6-4T No 80013, formerly of 70F Bournemouth, as it stands cold and still near to some wagons in the yard at 70D Eastleigh on 23rd June 1966. For many years it was based at 75F Tunbridge Wells in Kent and 75A Brighton in Sussex until making the move westwards to Bournemouth in June 1964. It was cut up at Kings of Norwich in December 1966. (D.Titheridge)

136) Only three members of the unique Bulleid designed SR Q1 Class 0-6-0's survived into 1966, Nos 33006/20/27, and all were withdrawn in the January from 70C Guildford. On 1st May 1966 No 33006 is captured by the photographer within the confines of the running shed at 70A Nine Elms in the company of an unidentified SR Light Pacific and BR Class 3 2-6-2T No 82026. No 33006 was eventually despatched to Cashmores, Newport for scrapping. (C.P.Stacey)

37) For many years a trio of LMS Class 5 4-6-0's, Nos 44693-95, were allocated to 56F Low Moor and by coincidence all three moved to 56D Mirfield together during April 1964. Again by 'coincidence' all three were back at Low Moor by November 1966. Whilst still based at 56D Mirfield, No 44694 is photographed near to the shed on 18th March 1966. No 44693 was withdrawn in May 1967, followed by No 44695 a month later with No 44694 surviving until October 1967. (N.E.Preedy)

38) By late 1963 there were no less than sixteen LNER A4 Class 4-6-2's allocated to depots in Scotland, Nos 60004/5/6/7/9/10/ 11/12/16/19/23/24/26/27/31/34. By the end of 1965 their ranks had been reduced to just seven, Nos 60004/7/9/19/24/26/34. On 18th July 1966 attention is given to one of the survivors by the driver of No 60034 *Lord Faringdon*, from 61B Aberdeen (Ferryhill)) as it heads a Glasgow to Aberdeen express at Stirling station. (R.Butterfield)

139) Clouds of smoke are blasted skywards from the funnel of former North Eastern Railway J27 Class 0-6-0 No 65795, from 52G Sunderland, as it powers a lengthy rake of mineral wagons towards the camera at Ryehope Grange Junction, Sunderland on 13th June 1967. No 65795 was withdrawn the following month and disposed of by Willoughbys of Choppington. (N.E.Preedy)

40) A trio of unidentified Stanier LMS locomotives are present within this photograph taken in the depot yard at 9D Newton Heath in October 1967. Also present is a BR 9F Class 2-10-0 its identity obscured by the fact that the numberplate is missing. The one engine we can identify is BR *Britannia* Class 4-6-2 No 70013 *Oliver Cromwell*, an inmate of 12A Carlisle (Kingmoor). When Kingmoor closed at the end of 1967, No 70013 moved to 10A Carnforth. (R.Butterfield)

41) Two electric multiple unit trains are within their lair at Wimbledon as SR Rebuilt *West Country* Class 4-6-2 No 34037 *Clovelly*, from 70D Eastleigh and in terrible external condition, heads the 18.20 hours Waterloo to Southampton Docks boat train on 8th July 1967. This was the last steam hauled train out of Waterloo and the last steam service train from a London terminus. Withdrawn the following day, *Clovelly* was eventually cut up in March 1968. (F.Hornby)

142) After the end of Southern Region steam a number of locations were earmarked as collecting points for stored locomotives prior to their being despatched for scrapping. One of these places was at 70E Salisbury, where, on 13th July 1967 a trio of engines await their sad, but inevitable fate. From left to right they are BR Class 4 2-6-4T No 80146 (ex. 70F Bournemouth), SR USA Class 0-6-0T No 30071 (ex. 70D Eastleigh) and BR Class 4 2-6-4T No 80152 (also 70D). (Mike Wood)

143) During the late fifties LMS Class 5 4-6-0 No 45377 was allocated to 10C/26F Patricroft shed in Manchester. In January 1960 it moved on to pastures new at 24F Fleetwood and then later in the same year to 24E Blackpool, where it remained for a number of years. In September 1964 it was on the move again, this time to 9M Bury. In April 1965 it moved to a final abode at 9K Bolton where it is seen in steam in the yard in August 1967. (H.L.Holland)

14) Although taken out of normal revenue earning service by the motive power authorities at 61B Aberdeen (Ferryhill) in September 1966, LNER A4 Class 4-6-2 No 60019 *Bittern*, built at Doncaster Works in 1937, was immediately earmarked for preservation. It is photographed at Guide Bridge with the MRTS 'Mancunian' railtour on a damp and miserable 25th November 1967. Once of 52A Gateshead, *Bittern* was transferred to Ferryhill in November 1963. (N.E.Preedy)

15) A few short weeks from the end of steam on the Southern and we find SR USA Class 0-6-0T No 30064 hard at work shunting wagons in the marshalling yard at Basingstoke on 18th May 1967. As with the other thirteen members of the class, No 30064 was allocated to 71I Southampton Docks in its earlier days. From June 1963 (apart from a brief spell on loan at Meldon Quarry) it was based at 70D Eastleigh and was withdrawn in July 1967. (D.Titheridge)

146) A snowy scene at Canklow shed in February 1967. Although there are some wagons posted by the coaling plant the depot had been closed for well over twelve months. Once owned by the Midland Railway, Canklow was coded 19C by the London Midland Region authorities and 41D by the Eastern Region ones under BR. On the date this photo was taken it was used as a storage point for several locos including LMS Tank engines Nos 41533, 41708 and 41734. (R.Butterfield)

147) The 10.17am express from Leeds to Carlisle is well patronised by railway enthusiasts judging the numbers of heads seen poking out of windows in the carriages on 26th August 1967. The subject of vast interest is the locomotive in charge of the train, seen here at Skipton, LMS *Jubilee* Class 4-6-0 No 45562 *Alberta*, from 55A Leeds (Holbeck). After withdrawal from Holbeck in November 1967, *Alberta* was later cut up at Cashmores, Great Bridge. (D.Webster)

48) Although a duet of English Electric Type 3 diesels are present in this picture it is not quite the end of the road for LNER Kl Class 2-6-0 No 62045 seen out of steam in the shed yard at 51C West Hartlepool on 11th June 1967. The following month it was drafted to 52H Tyne Dock where it continued to work on freight trains for two months or so. It was finally condemned during September 1967 and scrapped at Hughes Bolckows, North Blyth. (R.W.Hinton)

49) Late British Railways transfers brought the unusual sight of lined green BR Class 5 4-6-0's like No 73026 onto the books of the shed at 9K Bolton. No 73026, once of the Western Region and based at 86C Cardiff (Canton)) found its way to Bolton in May 1966 via 6E Chester (GWR) 84G Shrewsbury, 2L Leamington Spa and 2A Tyseley. Its life at Bolton was only brief and in this picture it is noted on the scrapline on 16th April 1967 with a sister engine. (H.L.Holland)

150) With a diesel multiple unit invading the picture, BR Class 2 2-6-0 No 78037 (10D Lostock Hall) looks the worse for wear as it performs as a station pilot at Preston station on a drab looking 1st April 1967, a month before condemnation. Throughout most of its working life No 78037 was employed at various depots in the north west including 10B/24K Preston, 24G/10G Skipton and 8F Springs Branch Wigan. It was cut up at a scrapyard in Motherwell. (T.R.Amos)

151) With the west end of Bournemouth (Central) in the background, BR Class 4 2-6-0 No 76011 stands at bufferstops near to the turntable at its home shed at 70F on 19th February 1967. Although out of steam, No 76011 still had several months of work ahead at Bournemouth. This locomotive came to 70F by way of 71A/70D Eastleigh (twice), and 72C Yeovil. After condemnation in July 1967 it was despatched to 70E Salisbury prior to scrapping. (Mike Wood)

52) To say that the infrastructure of the depot at 52H Tyne Dock was in a state of 'disrepair' on 14th June 1967 would be a slight understatement. As closure was on the immediate horizon it is doubtful if anyone cared about its well being, least of all the 'mandarins' on the British Railways board. In steam between two roundhouses is locally based LNER Q6 Class 0-8-0 No 63387 which was reallocated to 51C West Hartlepool in July 1967. (N.E.Preedy)

53) Dark shadows are cast by the large overbridge at Manchester (Victoria) station on a cold and dismal 16th December 1967. Lurking behind the bridge portals are two LMS Class 8F 2-8-0's Nos 48380 and 48773, both from 9K Bolton. By this stage in time the only major cities which hosted steam were Carlisle, Liverpool and Manchester. Both Nos 48380 and 48773 were condemned in the summer of 1968, but the latter was saved by the Severn Valley Railway. (D.K.Jones)

154) The rustic tranquility of the wooded countryside near to Middlewich on former London and North Western metals in Cheshire, is disturbed momentarily by the passing of BR Class 9F 2-10-0 No 92058, from 8B Warrington, which is being employed on an enthusiasts special on 29th April 1967. The station at Middlewich, situated between Northwich and Sandbach, closed in 1960. No 92058 followed suit in October 1967, from 12A Carlisle (Kingmoor). (B.J.Miller)

155) The white exhaust from the chimney of 12A Carlisle (Kingmoor) allocated Stanier LMS Class 5 4-6-0 No 45259 is highlighted by weak sunshine as it powers a fitted freight at Warrington on the West Coast Main Line in January 1967. This locomotive was a favourite in the Carlisle area being based at both Upperby and Kingmoor sheds until its withdrawal in December 1967. It was cut up by Wards of Beighton, Sheffield in April 1968. (Kit Windle)

56) The former London and South Western Railway shed at 70D Basingstoke lost its parent status in March 1963, becoming a sub-shed of 71A Eastleigh. Despite the downgrading it continued to service steam locomotives until the bitter end in July 1967. Alongside the small straight running structure on 18th March 1967 are an unidentified BR Class 5 4-6-0 and BR Class 4 2-6-4T No 80139, from 70D Eastleigh, which also survived until the end of Southern steam. (R.W.Hinton)

57) Sunlight and shadow outside 9K Bolton in August 1967 where a bedraggled but defiant LMS Class 8F 2-8-0 No 48559 has a short, but useful life ahead of it. Once a longstanding inmate at 2A/1F Rugby, No 48559 also served at 1A Willesden and 5B Crewe (South) before moving to Bolton in August 1967. Withdrawn from the latter in January 1968 it lay in store there for three months before being transported to Drapers, Hull for scrapping. (H.L.Holland)

158) The awesome looking monolithic concrete coaling plant at 10D Lostock Hall still had six months of use ahead of it when this photgraph was taken on 2nd February 1968. In steam beneath it is one of the last surviving Ivatt LMS Class 4 2-6-0's No 43027 a resident of Lostock Hall. Although in work-stained condition the number and smokebox plates have been smartened up. It was rendered redundant by the shed authorities in May 1968. (N.E.Preedy)

159) The end is nigh for Stanier LMS Class 8F 2-8-0 No 48323 pictured here in the shed yard at 10F Rose Grove on 3rd June 1968, the same month that it was withdrawn. No 48323 had been a resident of Rose Grove since moving here from 8H Birkenhead in May 1965. Other locations for No 48323 from the late fifties onwards were at 8C Speke Junction, 8D Widnes, 6B Mold Junction and 8A Edge Hill (Liverpool). It was cut up at Drapers, Hull in December 1968. (C.P.Stacey)

160) All is desolate and silent at 10A Carnforth in September 1968 one month after the shed closed. Until the depot was established as a live preservation centre the sounds and smells of steam engines being prepared for duty or at rest would be a thing of the past. Awaiting the final call to the scrapyard are two LMS Class 5 4-6-0's Nos 45095 and 45445 along with BR Class 9F 2-10-0 No 92091. All were condemned between June and August 1968. (D.K.Jones)

161) A view of the depot at 10D Lostock Hall with its eight roads (looking eastwards) with steam a'plenty along with water columns, a brazier and other bric-a-brac present on 2nd February 1968. In the left of the frame is LMS Class 5 4-6-0 No 44672, once a longstanding resident of 12A Carlisle (Kingmoor), an unidentified LMS Class 8F 2-8-0 in the centre of the frame and on the right is LMS Class 5 4-6-0 No 44816, an inmate of Lostock Hall since October 1967. (N.E.Preedy)

162) This busy scene taken at Rose Grove West, with the depot in the background, could give an illusion that it was taken at the height of steam dominance, but unfortunately it was in its eleventh hour. On view is a Warwickshire Railway Society special which has halted at Rose Grove. In charge of the train and both in immaculate condition, are LMS Class 5 4-6-0 No 44949 (9D Newton Heath) and BR Class 5 4-6-0 No 73069 (9H Patricroft) on 18th May 1968. (N.E.Preedy)

163) A section of the depot yard at 9E Trafford Park in Manchester two months or so after total closure. Present on 26th May 1968 are four LMS Class 5 4-6-0's all stripped of their motion. Facing the camera are Nos 44895 (withdrawn in December 1967) and No 45258 (withdrawn in March 1968). This scene is a dismal one compared to the days when Trafford Park had LMS *Patriot*, *Jubilee* and *Royal Scot* Class 4-6-0's on its books, along with BR *Britannia* Pacifics. (F.Hornby)

164) Although sporting a 26A shedplate (used as the code for Newton Heath until September 1963) LMS Class 5 4-6-0 No 45350 is a visitor to 9K Bolton from 10F Rose Grove on 16th June 1968 During the late fifties No 45350 was allocated to 1A Willesden until moving north to 5D Stoke in July 1960. It remained at Stoke for several years before being drafted to 8F Springs Branch Wigan. It was condemned from Rose Grove in early August 1968. (N.E.Preedy)

165) In stark contrast to the gloomy picture on page 89 (163) there is 'live' steam on shed at 9D Newton Heath on 6th April 1968. Refuelled and ready for their next duties are two LMS Class 5 4-6-0's Nos 44809 and 44845, both inmates at Newton Heath. When the depot closed to steam at the end of June No 44845 was condemned, but No 44809 was despatched to 10A Carnforth. After withdrawal in August, No 44809 became another victim of Drapers, Hull. (Mike Wood)

166) Another surviving LMS Class 5 4-6-0 No 44971 is noted at Preston station on 28th April 1968 whilst waiting to take over an express. Allocated to 10D Lostock Hall from 6D Shrewsbury in September 1966, No 44971 had spent much of its latter years based at depots on the North Wales Main Line, these being at 6B Mold Junction (twice), 6J Holyhead, 6A Chester and 6G Llandudno Junction. Yet again Drapers claimed the remains. (R.W.Hinton)

(67) We can just decipher a part of a chalked slogan 'Gone but not forgotten' on the tender of LMS Class 8F 2-8-0 No 48017, latterly of 8A Edge Hill (Liverpool), which was withdrawn from there at the end of 1967, as it stands amidst other condemned steam locomotives at 8C Speke Junction on 6th April 1968. Once of 8D Widnes, 8E Northwich, 8H Birkenhead and 8L Aintree, No 48017 (partially stripped of motion) was cut up in July 1968. (Mike Wood)

(68) We complete these memories of BR Steaming Through The Sixties - Volume 15 with this photograph taken at 10D Lostock Hall on 6th April 1968. In the left of the frame we can just make out the front end of an LMS Class 4 2-6-0. In the centre of the picture are LMS Class 5 4-6-0 No 45345 and LMS Class 8F 2-8-0 No 48253. No 45345 was destined to die at Lostock Hall in June 1968 followed by No 48253 two months later, along with the shed. (Mike Wood)

169) Complete with shed and numberplates GWR 9400 Class 0-6-0PT No 9420, withdrawn from 81A Old Oak Common the previous month, stands in the scrap line at Swindon Works on 26th April 1964. Constructed in June 1950 this Hawksworth designed locomotive spent its short working life in the London area based initially at 81D Reading and latterly at Old Oak where it no doubt spent most of its time moving empty coaching stock in and out of Paddington. (Tim Farebrother)

170) Once steam withdrawals began in earnest the railway workshops could not cope with the vast numbers of steam engines which were due for scrapping, so many were sent to private scrapyards like this one at Birds, Long Marston near to Stratford-upon-Avon. Awaiting their turn for cutting up on 27th November 1965 are LMS Class 6P5F 2-6-0 No 42905 (withdrawn from 9D Newton Heath in July 1965) and LMS Class 4F 0-6-0 No 44076. (C.Richards)

71) Another contractors scrapyard was at Cox and Danks, Wadsley Bridge on the outskirts of Sheffield where many steam locomotives were disposed of. Standing amidst the weeds on 5th November 1965 is the rusting hulk of War Department Class 8F 2-8-0 No 90340, taken out of traffic at 41E Staveley Barrow Hill in July 1965. Note the coupling rod which is strapped to the boiler. No 90340 once served at 31B March and 36A Doncaster. (R.Turner)

72) Three months after being condemned from 51L Thornaby we espy LNER A8 Class 4-6-2T No 69869 waiting for the cutter's torch at Darlington scrapyard on 4th September 1960. This engine was the prototype of the class, rebuilt from the LNER H1 Class 4-4-4 Tanks and it remained as an individual example for a number of years before the rest of the class was rebuilt. Note that No 69869 has a cage bunker with a hopper unlike sister engine No 69860 standing behind. (N.L.Browne)

CHAPTER ELEVEN - PRESERVED LOCOMOTIVES

173) A 'triple-header' at Winchcombe station on the Gloucestershire and Warwickshire preserved railway on the occasion of the autumn steam gala on 17th October 1993. Leading the charge with a Toddington to Gretton train is LNER A3 Class 4-6-2 No 60103 *Flying Scotsman* along with GWR *Modified Hall* Class 4-6-0 No 6998 *Burton Agnes Hall* and LMS Class 2 2-6-0 No 46521. (R.W Hinton)

174) The long preserved veteran of the Highland Railway, Jones Goods 4-6-0 No 103 is captured by the camera at Forres during the Highland Centenary week with a special from Inverness involving the use of two restored coaches on 25th August 1965. (N.E. Preedy)

175) Although no date is given by the photographer, this picture is taken during the early days of the Severn Valley Railway (how the landscape has changed since) at Bridgnorth. A mother stands near to the footbridge with her young son as they admire the ouline of LMS Ivatt Class 2 2-6-0 No 46443 and GWR 2251 Class 0-6-0 No 3205 (R.Butterfield)